C000097713

POEMS *of the* GREAT WAR

An Anthology
1914–1918

POEMS *of the* GREAT WAR
An Anthology 1914–1918

Edited by
Christopher Navratil

RUNNING PRESS
PHILADELPHIA · LONDON

9 8 7 6 5 4 3 2
Digit on the right indicates the number of this printing
Library of Congress Control Number: 2013934594
ISBN 978-0-7624-5088-6

Running Press Book Publishers
A Member of the Perseus Books Group
2300 Chestnut Street
Philadelphia, PA 19103-4371

Visit us on the web!
www.runningpress.com

Introduction

The poets of World War I, "The Great War," continue to hold a distinctive place in modern English literature. This generation of "Soldier Poets" was eager to reveal the brutal realities of war in an honest and straightforward manner. Eschewing the romanticized themes and language of the Victorian poets, their writing emerged as reportage with a new style that was unadorned, immediate. What had once been celebrated as a courageous military feat in a poem like Tennyson's "The Charge of the Light Brigade" was now transformed to a heartless depiction of humanity in Wilfred Owen's "Anthem of Doomed Youth"—"What passing-bells for these who die as cattle?" Underscoring the soulless nature of the modern industrial era, this new generation's bleak message was clear: war is merciless, death is senseless.

At the height of the war, this stark poetry was immensely popular. Hundreds of thousands of poems were written and published in those years between 1914 and 1918. Yet only a few hundred poems have endured. Most of the poets represented in this anthology experienced the war firsthand, part of a crop of well-educated young men serving in battle, often with literary aspirations. The careers of a few such as

Siegfried Sassoon, Robert
Graves, Ivor Gurney, and
Herbert Read were launched,
their reputations enduring
throughout much of the
twentieth century. Yet tragically,
several others were killed
in battle or died of disease or
infection: Rupert Brooke,
Charles Hamilton Sorley,
Edward Thomas, Isaac
Rosenberg, Wilfred Owen,
John McCrae; their talent and
immense potential woefully cut
short. Even the older men who

did not serve in combat—
already-established writers like
Rudyard Kipling and Thomas
Hardy—were deeply affected by
loss, overcome by the sense of
despair that permeated the
consciousness of the country.
"Sorrows manifold," Hardy
wrote on the signing of the
Armistice, November 11, 1918,
"Among the young, among the
weak and old, And the pensive
Spirit of Pity whispered, 'Why?'"

John Masefield
(1878–1967)

August, 1914
John Masefield

How still this quiet
    cornfield is to-night!
By an intenser glow the
    evening falls,

Bringing, not darkness, but
   a deeper light;
Among the stooks a
   partridge covey calls.

The windows glitter on the
   distant hill;
Beyond the hedge the
   sheep-bells in the fold
Stumble on sudden music
   and are still;
The forlorn pine woods
   droop above the wold.

An endless quiet valley
   reaches out
Past the blue hills into the
   evening sky;
Over the stubble, cawing,
   goes a rout
Of rooks from harvest,
   flagging as they fly.

So beautiful it is, I never
    saw
So great a beauty on these
    English fields
Touched by the twilight's
    coming into awe,
Ripe to the soul and rich
    with summer's yields. . . .

These homes, this valley
    spread below me here,
The rooks, the titled stacks,
    the beasts in pen,

Have been the heartfelt
    things, past speaking dear
To unknown generations of
    dead men,

❖ ❖ ❖

Who, century after century,
    held these farms,
And, looking out to watch
    the changing sky,
Heard, as we hear, the
    rumours and alarms
Of war at hand and danger
    pressing nigh.

And knew, as we know, that
   the message meant
The breaking off of ties, the
   loss of friends,
Death like a miser getting in
   his rent,
And no new stones laid
   where the trackway ends.

The harvest not yet won,
   the empty bin,

The friendly horses taken
   from the stalls,
The fallow on the hill not
   yet brought in,
The cracks unplastered in
   the leaking walls.

Yet heard the news, and
   went discouraged home,
And brooded by the fire
   with heavy mind,
With such dumb loving of
   the Berkshire loam

As breaks the dumb hearts
  of the English kind,

❖ ❖ ❖

Then sadly rose and left the
  well-loved Downs,
And so by ship to sea, and
  knew no more
The fields of home, the
  byres, the market towns,
Nor the dear outline of the
  English shore,

But knew the misery of the
    soaking trench,
The freezing in the rigging,
    the despair
In the revolting second of
    the wrench
When the blind soul is flung
    upon the air,

❖ ❖ ❖

And died (uncouthly, most)
    in foreign lands
For some idea but dimly
    understood

Of an English city never
   built by hands
Which love of England
   prompted and made
   good. . . .

❖ ❖ ❖

If there be any life beyond
   the grave,
It must be near the men and
   things we love,
Some power of quick
   suggestion how to save,

Touching the living soul as
   from above.

An influence from the Earth
   from those dead hearts
So passionate once, so deep,
   so truly kind,
That in the living child the
   spirit starts,
Feeling companioned still,
   not left behind.

Surely above these fields a
   spirit broods

A sense of many watchers
     muttering near,
Of the lone Downland with
     the forlorn woods
Loved to the death,
     inestimably dear.

❖ ❖ ❖

A muttering from beyond
     the veils of Death
From long-dead men, to
     whom this quiet scene
Came among blinding tears
     with the last breath,

The dying soldier's vision of
    his queen.

All the unspoken worship of
    those lives
Spent in forgotten wars at
    other calls
Glimmers upon these fields
    where evening drives
Beauty like breath, so
    gently darkness falls.

Darkness that makes the
   meadows holier still,
The elm trees sadden in the
   hedge, a sigh
Moves in the beech clump
   on the haunted hill,
The rising planets deepen
   in the sky,

❖ ❖ ❖

And silence broods like
   spirit on the brae,
A glimmering moon begins,
   the moonlight runs

Over the grasses of the
    ancient way
Rutted this morning by the
    passing guns.
—1914

Rudyard Kipling
(1865–1936)

For All We
Have and Are
Rudyard Kipling

For all we have and are,
For all our children's fate,
Stand up and take the war.
The Hun is at the gate!

Our world has passed away,
In wantonness o'erthrown.
There is nothing left to-day
But steel and fire and stone!

❖ ❖ ❖

Though all we knew depart,
The old Commandments
    stand:
"In courage keep your
    heart,
In strength lift up your
    hand."

Once more we hear the
  word
That sickened earth of
  old: —
"No law except the Sword
Unsheathed and
  uncontrolled."
Once more it knits
  mankind,
Once more the nations go
To meet and break and bind
A crazed and driven foe.

Comfort, content, delight—
The ages' slow-bought
    gain—
They shrivelled in a night.
Only ourselves remain
To face the naked days
In silent fortitude,
Through perils and dismays
Renewed and re-renewed.

Though all we made depart,
The old Commandments
    stand:

"In patience keep your
 heart,
In strength life up your
 hand."

❖ ❖ ❖

No easy hope or lies
Shall bring us to our goal,
But iron sacrifice
Of body, will, and soul.
There is but one task for
 all—

Rudyard Kipling

One life for each to give.
Who stands if Freedom fall?
Who dies if England live?
—1914

Rupert Brooke
(1887–1915)

The Soldier
Rupert Brooke

If I should die, think only
    this of me:
That there's some corner
    of a foreign field

That is for ever England.
   There shall be
In that rich earth a richer
   dust concealed;
A dust whom England bore,
   shaped, made aware,
Gave, once, her flowers to
   love, her ways to roam,
A body of England's,
   breathing English air,
Washed by the rivers, blest
   by suns of home.

And think, this heart, all
   evil shed away,
A pulse in the eternal mind,
   no less
Gives somewhere back the
   thoughts by England
   given;
Her sights and sounds;
   dreams happy as her day;
And laughter, learnt of
   friends; and gentleness,
In hearts at peace, under an
   English heaven.
—1915

Fragment
Rupert Brooke

I strayed about the deck, an
   hour, to-night
Under a cloudy moonless
   sky; and peeped
In at the windows, watched
   my friends at table,
Or playing cards, or
   standing in the doorways,

Or coming out into the
   darkness. Still
No one could see me.

I would have thought of
   them
—Heedless, within a week
   of battle—in pity,
Pride in their strength and
   in the weight and
   firmness
And link'd beauty of bodies,
   and pity that

This gay machine of
   splendour'ld soon be
   broken,
Thought little of, pashed,
   scattered . . . .

❖ ❖ ❖

Only, always,
I could but see them—
   against the lamplight—
   pass
Like coloured shadows,
   thinner than filmy glass,

Slight bubbles, fainter than
   the wave's faint light,
That broke to phosphorus
   out in the night,
Perishing things and
   strange ghosts—soon to
   die
To other ghosts—this one,
   or that, or I.
—1915

Edward
Thomas
(1878–1917)

Fifty Faggots
Edward Thomas

There they stand, on their
ends, the fifty faggots
That once were underwood
of hazel and ash

In Jenny Pink's Copse. Now,
by the hedge
Close packed, they make a
thicket fancy alone
Can creep through with the
mouse and wren. Next
Spring
A blackbird or a robin will
nest there,
Accustomed to them,
thinking they will remain
Whatever is for ever to a
bird.

This Spring it is too late; the
   swift has come,
'Twas a hot day for carrying
   them up:
Better they will never warm
   me, though they must
Light several Winters' fires.
   Before they are done
The war will have ended,
   many other things
Have ended, maybe, that I
   can no more

Foresee or more control
than robin and wren.
—1915

This Is No Case of Petty Right or Wrong
Edward Thomas

This is no case of petty right
    or wrong
That politicians or
    philosophers
Can judge. I hate not
    Germans, not grow hot
With love of Englishmen, to
    please newspapers.

Beside my hate for one fat
    patriot
My hatred of the Kaiser is
    love true: —
A kind of god he is, banging
    a gong.
But I have not to choose
    between the two,
Or between justice and
    injustice. Dinned
With war and argument I
    read no more

Than in the storm smoking
   along the wind
Athwart the wood. Two
   witches' cauldrons roar.
From one the weather shall
   rise clear and gay;
Out of the other an England
   beautiful
And like her mother that
   died yesterday.
Little I know or care if,
   being dull,

I shall miss something that
    historians
Can take out of the ashes
    when perchance
The phoenix broods serene
    above their ken.
But with the best and
    meanest Englishmen
I am one in crying, God save
    England, lest
We lose what never slaves
    and cattle blessed.

The ages made her that
   made us from dust:
She is all we know and live
   by, and we trust
She is good and must
   endure, loving her so:
And as we love ourselves we
   hate her foe.
—1915

Lights Out
Edward Thomas

I have come to the borders
    of sleep
The unfathomable deep
Forest where all must lose
Their way, however
    straight,
Or winding, soon or late;
They cannot choose.

Many a road and track
That, since the dawn's first
   crack,
Up to the forest brink,
Deceived the travellers,
Suddenly now blurs,
And in they sink.

❖ ❖ ❖

Here love ends,
Despair, ambition ends,
All pleasure and all trouble,
Although most sweet or
   bitter,

Here ends in sleep that is
   sweeter
Than tasks most noble.

❖ ❖ ❖

There is not any book
Or face of dearest look
That I would not turn from
   now
To go into the unknown
I must enter and leave alone
I know not how.

Edward Thomas

The tall forest towers;
Its cloudy foliage lowers
Ahead, shelf above shelf;
Its silence I hear and obey
That I may lose my way
And myself.
—1916

The Owl
Edward Thomas

Downhill I came, hungry,
and yet not starved;
Cold, yet had heat within
me that was proof
Against the North wind;
tired, yet so that rest
Had seemed the sweetest
thing under a roof.

Then at the inn I had food,
    fire, and rest,
Knowing how hungry, cold,
    and tired was I.
All of the night was quite
    barred out except
An owl's cry, a most
    melancholy cry

Shaken out long and clear
    upon the hill,
No merry note, nor cause of
    merriment,

But one telling me plain
    what I escaped
And others could not, that
    night, as in I went.

❖ ❖ ❖

And salted was my food, and
    my repose,
Salted and sobered, too, by
    the bird's voice
Speaking for all who lay
    under the stars,
Soldiers and poor, unable to
    rejoice.
—1917

When First

Edward Thomas

When first I came here I
  had hope,
Hope for I knew not what.
  Fast beat
My heart at sight of the tall
  slope
Of grass and yews, as my
  feet

Only by scaling its steps of
    chalk
Would see something no
    other hill
Ever disclosed. And now I
    walk
Down it the last time. Never
    will

My heart beat so again at
    sight
Of any hill although as fair
And loftier. For infinite
The change, late
    unperceived, this year,

❖ ❖ ❖

The twelfth, suddenly,
    shows me plain.
Hope now, – not health, nor
    cheerfulness,
Since they can come and go
    again,

As often one brief hour
   witnesses, —

Just hope has gone for ever.
   Perhaps
I may love other hills yet
   more
Than this: the future and
   the maps
Hide something I was
   waiting for.

One thing I know, that love
   with chance
And use and time and
   necessity
Will grow, and louder the
   heart's dance
At parting than at meeting
   be.
—1917

John McCrae
(1872–1918)

In Flanders Fields
John McCrae

In Flanders fields the
    poppies blow
Between the crosses, row
    on row,

That mark our place; and in
   the sky
The larks, still bravely
   singing, fly
Scarce heard amid the guns
   below.

❖ ❖ ❖

We are the Dead. Short days
   ago
We lived, felt dawn, saw
   sunset glow,
Loved and were loved, and
   now we lie,
     In Flanders fields.

Take up our quarrel with
   the foe:
To you from failing hands
   we throw
The torch; be yours to hold
   it high.
If ye break faith with us
   who die
We shall not sleep, though
   poppies grow
      In Flanders fields.
—1915

Charles Hamilton Sorley

(1895–1915)

To Germany

Charles Hamilton Sorley

You are blind like us. Your
hurt no man designed,

And no man claimed the
    conquest of your land.
But gropers both through
    fields of thought confined
We stumble and we do not
    understand.
You only saw your future
    bigly planned,
And we, the tapering paths
    of our own mind,
And in each other's dearest
    ways we stand,

And hiss and hate. And the
blind fight the blind.

❖ ❖ ❖

When it is peace, then we
may view again
With new-won eyes each
other's truer form
And wonder. Grown more
loving-kind and warm
We'll grasp firm hands and
laugh at the old pain,

When it is peace. But until
  peace, the storm
The darkness and the
  thunder and the rain.
—1916

When You See Millions of the Mouthless Dead

Charles Hamilton Sorley

When you see millions of
the mouthless dead
Across your dreams in pale
battalions go,
Say not soft things as other
men have said,
That you'll remember. For
you need not so.

Give them not praise. For,
   deaf, how should they
   know
It is not curses heaped on
   each gashed head?
Nor tears. Their blind eyes
   see not your tears flow.
Nor honour. It is easy to be
   dead.
Say only this, 'They are
   dead.' Then add thereto,
'Yet many a better one has
   died before.'

Then, scanning all the
  o'ercrowded mass, should
  you
Perceive one face that you
  loved heretofore,
It is a spook. None wears
  the face you knew.
Great death has made all his
  for evermore.
—1916

Isaac Rosenberg
(1890–1918)

The Dead Heroes
Isaac Rosenberg

Flame out, you glorious
    skies,
Welcome, our brave,
Kiss their exultant eyes;
Give what they gave.

Flash, maile`d seraphin,
Your burning spears;
New days to outflame their
  dim
Heroic years.

❖ ❖ ❖

Thrills their baptismal
  tread
The bright proud air;
The embattled plumes
  outspread
Burn upwards there.

Flame out, flame out, O
   Song!
Star ring to star,
Strong as our hurt is strong
Our children are.

Their blood is England's
   heart;
By their dead hands
It is their noble part
That England stands.

England – Time gave them
    thee;
They gave back this
To win Eternity
And claim God's kiss.
—1914

Marching
(as seen from the left file)
Isaac Rosenberg

My eyes catch ruddy necks
Sturdily pressed back—
All a red brick moving glint,
Like flaming pendulums, hands
Swing across the khaki—
Mustard coloured khaki—
To the automatic feet.

We husband the ancient
   glory
In these bared necks and
   hands.
Not broke is the forge of
   Mars;
But a subtler brain beats
   iron
To shoe the hoofs of death,
(Who paws dynamic air
   now).

Blind fingers loose an iron
    cloud
To rain immortal darkness
On strong eyes.
—1915

From France
Isaac Rosenberg

The spirit drank the Café
    lights;
All the hot life that glittered
    there,
And heard men say to
    women gay,
'Life is not Life in France'.

The spirit dreams of Café
    lights,

And golden faces and soft
  tones,
And hears men groan to
  broken men,
'This is not Life in France'.

Heaped stones and a
  charred signboard shows
With grass between and
  dead folk under,
And some birds sing, while
  the spirit takes wing.
And this is life in France.
—1916

Returning, We Hear the Larks

Isaac Rosenberg

Sombre the night is.
And though we have our
    lives, we know
What sinister threat lurks
    there.

Dragging these anguished
    limbs, we only know

This poison-blasted track
  opens on our camp –
On a little safe sleep.

But hark! joy—joy – strange
  joy.
Lo! heights of night ringing
  with unseen larks.
Music showering on our
  upturned list'ning faces.

Isaac Rosenberg

Death could drop from the
    dark
As easily as song –
But song only dropped,
Like a blind man's dreams
    on the sand
By dangerous tides,
Like a girl's dark hair for she
    dreams no ruin lies there,
Or her kisses where a
    serpent hides.
—1917

Richard Aldington
(1882–1962)

Bombardment
Richard Aldington

Four days the earth was
    rent and torn
By bursting steel,
The houses fell about us;

Three nights we dared not
  sleep,
Sweating, and listening for
  the imminent crash
Which meant our death.

The fourth night every man,
Nerve-tortured, racked to
  exhaustion,
Slept, muttering and
  twitching,
While the shells crashed
  overhead.

The fifth day there came a
    hush;
We left our holes
And looked above the
    wreckage of the earth
To where the white clouds
    moved in silent lines
Across the untroubled blue.
—1915

Wilfred Owen
(1893–1918)

Anthem for Doomed Youth
Wilfred Owen

What passing-bells for
these who die as cattle?
Only the monstrous anger
of the guns.

Only the stuttering rifles'
　　rapid rattle
Can patter out their hasty
　　orisons.
No mockeries for them; no
　　prayers nor bells,
Nor any voice of mourning
　　save the choirs, —
The shrill, demented choirs
　　of wailing shells;
And bugles calling for them
　　from sad shires.

What candles may be held
    to speed them all?
Not in the hands of boys,
    but in their eyes
Shall shine the holy
    glimmers of goodbyes.
The pallor of girls' brows
    shall be their pall;
Their flowers the
    tenderness of patient
    minds,
And each slow dusk a
    drawing-down of blinds.
—1917

Greater Love
Wilfred Owen

Red lips are not so red
As the stained stones kissed
    by the English dead.
Kindness of wooed and
    wooer
Seems shame to their love
    pure.
O Love, your eyes lose lure.
When I behold eyes blinded
    in my stead!

Your slender attitude
Trembles not exquisite like
    limbs knife-skewed,
Rolling and rolling there
Where God seems not to
    care;
Till the fierce love they bear
Cramps them in death's
    extreme decrepitude.

Your voice sings not so soft, —
Though even as wind
    murmuring through
    raftered loft, —
Your dear voice is not dear,
Gentle, and evening clear,
As theirs whom none now
    hear,
Now earth has stopped their
    piteous mouths that
    coughed.

Heart, you were never hot
Nor large, nor full like
    hearts made great with
    shot;
And though your hand be
    pale,
Paler are all which trail
Your cross through flame
    and hail:
Weep, you may weep, for
    you may touch them not.
—1918

Mental Cases
Wilfred Owen

Who are these? Why sit
   they here in twilight?
Wherefore rock they,
   purgatorial shadows,
Drooping tongues from
   jaws that slob their relish,
Baring teeth that leer like
   skulls' teeth wicked?
Stroke on stroke of pain, -
   but what slow panic,

Gouged these chasms round
    their fretted sockets?
Ever from their hair and
    through their hand palms
Misery swelters. Surely we
    have perished
Sleeping, and walk hell; but
    who these hellish?

—These are men whose
    minds the Dead have
    ravished.

Memory fingers in their
    hair of murders.
Multitudinous murders
    they once witnessed.
Wading sloughs of flesh
    these helpless wander,
Treading blood from lungs
    that had loved laughter.
Always they must see these
    things and hear them,
Batter of guns and shatter
    of flying muscles,

Carnage incomparable and
    human squander
Rucked too thick for these
    men's extrication.

❖ ❖ ❖

Therefore still their eyeballs
    shrink tormented
Back into their brains,
    because on their sense
Sunlight seems a blood-
    smear; night comes
    blood-black;
Dawn breaks open like a

wound that bleeds afresh
— Thus their heads wear
this hilarious, hideous,
Awful falseness of set-
smiling corpses.
— Thus their hands are
plucking at each other;
Picking at the rope-knouts
of their scourging;
Snatching after us who
smote them, brother,
Pawing us who dealt them
war and madness.
—1918

Spring Offensive
Wilfred Owen

Halted against the shade of
    a last hill,
They fed, and, lying easy,
    were at ease
And, finding comfortable
    chests and knees
Carelessly slept. But many
    there stood still
To face the stark, blank sky
    beyond the ridge,

Knowing their feet had
    come to the end of the
    world.

Marvelling they stood, and
    watched the long grass
    swirled
By the May breeze,
    murmurous with wasp
    and midge,
For though the summer
    oozed into their veins

Like the injected drug for
    their bones' pains,
Sharp on their souls hung
    the imminent line of
    grass,
Fearfully flashed the sky's
    mysterious glass.

Hour after hour they
    ponder the warm field –
And the far valley behind,
    where the buttercups
Had blessed with gold their

    slow boots coming up,
Where even the little
    brambles would not yield,
But clutched and clung to
    them like sorrowing
    hands;
They breathe like trees
    unstirred.

Till like a cold gust thrilled
    the little word
At which each body and its
    soul begird

And tighten them for battle.
   No alarms
Of bugles, no high flags, no
   clamorous haste —
Only a lift and flare of eyes
   that faced
The sun, like a friend with
   whom their love is done.
O larger shone that smile
   against the sun, —
Mightier than his whose
   bounty these have
   spurned.

So, soon they topped the
   hill, and raced together
Over an open stretch of
   herb and heather
Exposed. And instantly the
   whole sky burned
With fury against them; and
   soft sudden cups
Opened in thousands for
   their blood; and the green
   slopes
Chasmed and steepened
   sheer to infinite space.

Of them who running on
    that last high place
Leapt to swift unseen
    bullets, or went up
On the hot blast and fury of
    hell's upsurge.
Or plunged and fell away
    past this world's verge,
Some say God caught them
    even before they fell.

But what say such as from
    existence' brink
Ventured but drave too
    swift to sink.
The few who rushed in the
    body to enter hell,
And there out-fiending all
    its fiends and flames
With superhuman
    inhumanities,
Long-famous glories,
    immemorial shames —

And crawling slowly back,
    have by degree
Regained cool peaceful air
    in wonder —
Why speak they not of
    comrades that went
    under?
—1918

Wilfred Gibson
(1878–1962)

Air-Raid
Wilfred Gibson

Night shatters in mid-
    heaven: the bark of guns,
The roar of planes, the
    crash of bombs, and all
The unshackled skiey

pandemonium stuns
The senses to indifference,
    when a fall
Of masonry nearby startles
    awake,
Tingling, wide-eyed,
    prick-eared, with
    bristling hair,
Each sense within the body,
    crouched aware
Like some sore-hunted
    creature in the brake.

Yet side by side we lie in the
    little room
Just touching hands, with
    eyes and ears that strain
Keenly, yet dream-
    bewildered, through
    tense gloom,
Listening, in helpless
    stupor of insane
Cracked nightmares panic,
    fantastically wild,
To the quiet breathing of
    our sleeping child.
—1919

Ivor Gurney
(1890–1937)

To the Poet Before Battle
Ivor Gurney

Now, Youth, the hour of thy
dread passion comes,
Thy lovely things must all
be laid away;

And thou, as others, must
    face the riven day
Unstirred by the tattle and
    rattle of rolling drums,
Or bugles' strident cry.
    When mere noise numbs
The sense of being, the
    fear-sick soul doth sway,
Remember thy great craft's
    honour, that they may say
Nothing in shame of Poets.
    Then the crumbs

Ivor Gurney

Of praise the little
    versemen joyed to take
Shall be forgotten; then
    they must know we are,
For all our skill in words,
    equal in might
And strong of mettle as
    those we honoured; make
The name of Poet terrible in
    just War,
And like a crown of honour
    upon the fight.
—1915

Pain
Ivor Gurney

Pain, pain continued; pain
    unending;
Hard even to the roughest,
    but to those
Hungry for beauty ... Not
    the wisest knows,
Nor most pitiful-hearted,
    what the wending
Of one hour's way meant.
    Grey monotony lending

Weight to the grey skies,
   grey mud where goes
An army of grey bedrenched
   scarecrows in rows
Careless at last of cruellest
   Fate-sending.
Seeing the pitiful eyes of
   men foredone,
Or horses shot, too tired
   merely to stir,
Dying in shell-holes both,
   slain by the mud.

Men broken, shrieking even
    to hear a gun. —
Till pain grinds down, or
    lethargy numbs her,
The amazed heart cries
    angrily out on God.
—1917

The Dearness of Common Things

Ivor Gurney

The dearness of common
   things,
Beech wood, tea, plate
   shelves,
And the whole family of
   crockery,
Woodaxes, blades, helves.

Ivory milk, earth's coffee,
The white face of books
And the touch, feel, smell of
    paper,
Latin's lovely looks.

Earth fine to handle.
The touch of clouds
When the imagined arm
    leaps out to caress
Grey worsted or wool
    clouds.

Wool, rope, cloth, old pipes
Gone warped in service
And the one herb of tobacco,
The herb of grace, the censer
    weed
Of blue whorls, finger-traced
    curves —
The touch of sight how
    strange and marvellous
To any blind man pierced
    through his opaque,
When concrete objects grow.
—1919–1922

The Target
Ivor Gurney

I shot him, and it had to be
One of us! "Twas him or me.
Couldn't be helped,' and
   none can blame
Me, for you would do the
   same.

My mother, she can't sleep
   for fear
Of what might be
   a-happening here
To me. Perhaps it might be
   best
To die, and set her fears at
   rest.

For worst is worst, and
   worry's done.
Perhaps he was the only
   son . . .

Yet God keeps still, and
   does not say
A word of guidance any way.

❖ ❖ ❖

Well, if they get me, first I'll
   find
That boy, and tell him all
   my mind,
And see who felt the bullet
   worst,
And ask his pardon, if I
   durst.

All's a tangle. Here's my job.
A man might rave, or shout,
    or sob;
And God He takes no sort of
    heed.
This is a bloody mess
    indeed.
—1917

First Time In
Ivor Gurney

After the dread tales and
   red yarns of the Line
Anything might have come
   to us; but the divine
Afterglow brought us up to
   a Welsh colony
Hiding in sandbag ditches,
   whispering consolatory
Soft foreign things. Then we
   were taken in

To low huts candle-lit,
    shaded close by slitten
Oilsheets, and there the
    boys gave us kind
    welcome;
So that we looked out as
    from the edge of home.
Sang us Welsh things, and
    changed all former
    notions
To human hopeful things.
    And the next day's guns

Nor any line-pangs ever
   quite could blot out
That strangely beautiful
   entry to war's rout;
Candles they gave us,
   precious and shared
   over-rations —
Ulysses found little more in
   his wanderings without
   doubt.
'David of the White Rock',
   the 'Slumber Song' so
   soft, and that

Beautiful tune to which
    roguish words by Welsh
    pit boys
Are sung — but never more
    beautiful than here under
    the guns' noise.
—1916

Robert Graves
(1895–1985)

When I'm Killed
Robert Graves

When I'm killed, don't think
of me
Buried there in Cambrin
Wood,

Nor as in Zion think of me
With the Intolerable Good.
And there's one thing that I
   know well,
I'm damned if I'll be
   damned to Hell!

So when I'm killed, don't
   wait for me,
Walking the dim corridor;
In Heaven or Hell, don't
   wait for me,

Or you must wait for
    evermore.
You'll find me buried,
    living-dead
In these verses that you've
    read.

❖ ❖ ❖

So when I'm killed, don't
    mourn for me,
Shot, poor lad, so bold and
    young,
Killed and gone – don't
    mourn for me.

On your lips my life is hung:
O friends and lovers, you
   can save
Your playfellow from the
   grave.
—1916

The Assault Heroic

Robert Graves

Down in the mud I lay,
Tired out by my long day
Of five damned days and
  nights,
Five sleepless days and
  nights, . . .
Dream-snatched, and set
  me where

The dungeon of Despair
Looms over Desolate Sea,
Frowning and threatening
    me
With aspect high and
    steep —
A most malignant keep.
My foes that lay within
Shouted and made a din,
Hooted and grinned and
    cried:
"Today we've killed your
    pride;

Today your ardour ends.
We've murdered all your
    friends;
We've undermined by
    stealth
Your happiness and your
    health.
We've taken away your
    hope;
Now you may droop and
    mope
To misery and to Death.'
But with my spear of Faith,

Stout as an oaken rafter,
With my round shield of
    laughter,
With my sharp, tongue-like
    sword
That speaks a bitter word,
I stood beneath the wall
And there defied them all.
The stones they cast I
    caught
And alchemized with
    thought
Into such lumps of gold

As dreaming misers hold.
The boiling oil they threw
Fell in a shower of dew,
Refreshing me; the spears
Flew harmless by my ears,
Struck quivering in the sod;
There, like the prophet's
   rod,
Put leaves out, took firm
   root,
And bore me instant fruit.
My foes were all astounded,
Dumbstricken and

    confounded,
Gaping in a long row;
They dared not thrust nor
    throw.
Thus, then, I climbed a
    steep
Buttress and won the keep,
And laughed and proudly
    blew
My horn, 'Stand to! Stand
    to!
Wake up, sir! Here's a new
Attack! Stand to! Stand to!'
—1918

Corporal Stare
Robert Graves

Back from the line one
    night in June,
I gave a dinner at Bethune—
Seven courses, the most
    gorgeous meal
Money could buy or batman
    steal.
Five hungry lads welcomed
    the fish

With shouts that nearly
  cracked the dish;
Asparagus came with
  tender tops,
Strawberries in cream, and
  mutton chops,
Said Jenkins, as my hand he
  shook,
"They'll put this in the
  history book."
We bawled Church anthems
  in choro

Of Bethlehem and Hermon
   snow,
With drinking songs, a jolly
   sound
To help the good red
   Pommard round.
Stories and laughter
   interspersed,
We drowned a long La
   Bassée thirst—
Trenches in June make
   throats damned dry.

Then through the window
  suddenly,
Badge, stripes and medals
  all complete,
We saw him swagger up the
  street,
Just like a live man—
  Corporal Stare!
Stare! Killed last May at
  Festaubert.
Caught on patrol near the
  Boche wire,

Torn horribly by machine-
    gun fire!
He paused, saluted smartly,
    grinned,
Then passed away like a
    puff of wind,
Leaving us blank
    astonishment.
The song broke, up we
    started, leant
Out of the window—nothing
    there,

Not the least shadow of
  Corporal Stare,
Only a quiver of smoke that
  showed
A fag-end dropped on the
  silent road.
—1918

Recalling War
Robert Graves

Entrance and exit wounds
    are silvered clean,
The track aches only when
    the rain reminds.
The one-legged man forgets
    his leg of wood,
The one-armed man his
    jointed wooden arm.
The blinded man sees with
    his ears and hands

As much or more than once
    with both his eyes.
Their war was fought these
    twenty years ago
And now assumes the
    nature-look of time,
As when the morning
    traveller turns and views
His wild night-stumbling
    carved into a hill.

What then, was war? No
  mere discord of flags
But an infection of the
  common sky
That sagged ominously
  upon the earth
Even when the season was
  the airiest May.
Down pressed the sky, and
  we, oppressed, thrust out
Boastful tongue, clenched
  fist and valiant yard.

Natural infirmities were out
of mode,
For Death was young again;
patron alone
Of healthy dying,
premature fate-spasm.

❖ ❖ ❖

Fear made fine bed-fellows.
Sick with delight
At life's discovered
transitoriness,
Our youth became all-flesh
and waived the mind.

Never was such antiqueness
   of romance,
Such tasty honey oozing
   from the heart.
And old importances came
   swimming back —
Wine, meat, log-fires, a roof
   over the head,
A weapon at the thigh,
   surgeons at call.
Even there was a use again
   for God —

A word of rage in lack of
    meat, wine, fire,
In ache of wounds beyond
    all surgeoning.

❖ ❖ ❖

War was return of earth to
    ugly earth,
War was foundering of
    sublimities,
Extinction of each happy
    art and faith
By which the world had still
    kept head in air.

Protesting logic or
  protesting love,
Until the unendurable
  moment struck —
The inward scream, the
  duty to run mad.

And we recall the merry
  ways of guns —
Nibbling the walls of factory
  and church
Like a child, piecrust; felling
  groves of trees

Like a child, dandelions
    with a switch.
Machine-guns rattle
    toy-like from a hill,
Down in a row the brave
    tin-soldiers fall:
A sight to be recalled in
    elder days
When learnedly the future
    we devote
To yet more boastful visions
    of despair.
—1938

Harold Monro
(1878–1932)

Officers' Mess
Harold Monro

I search the room with all
my mind,
Peering among those eyes;
For I am feverish to find

A brain with which my
    brain may talk,
Not that I think myself too
    wise,
But that I'm lonely, and I
    walk
Round the large place and
    wonder. No —
There's nobody, I fear,
Lonely as I, and here.

How they hate me. I'm a
    fool:

I can't play Bridge; I'm bad
  at pool;
I cannot drone a comic son;
I can't talk shop; I can't use
  slang;
My jokes are bad, my stories
  long;
My voice will falter, break
  or hang,
Not blurt the sour sarcastic
  word—
And so my swearing sounds
  absurd.

But came the talk: I found
Three or four others for an
     argument.
I forced their pace. They
     shifted their dull ground,
And went
Sprawling about the
     passages of thought.
We tugged each other's
     words until they tore.
They asked me my
     philosophy: I brought
Bits of it forth and laid them
     on the floor.

They laughed, and so I
    kicked the bits about,
Then put them in my
    pocket one by one—
I sorry I had brought them
    out,
They grateful for the fun.

And when these words had
    thus been sent
Jerking about, like beetles
    round a wall,

Then one by one to dismal
    sleep we went.
There was no happiness at
    all
In that short hopeless
    argument
Through yawns and on the
    way to bed
Among men waiting to be
    dead.
—1916

Siegfried Sassoon
(1886–1967)

Counter-Attack
Siegfried Sassoon

We'd gained our first
    objective hours before
While dawn broke like a
    face with blinking eyes,

Pallid, unshaven and
   thirsty, blind with smoke.
Things seemed all right at
   first. We held their line,
With bombers posted,
   Lewis guns well placed,
And clink of shovels
   deepening the shallow
   trench.
The place was rotten with
   dead; green clumsy legs
High-booted, sprawled and
   grovelled along the saps;

And trunks, face downward,
    in the sucking mud,
Wallowed like trodden
    sand-bags loosely filled;
And naked sodden buttocks,
    mats of hair,
Bulged, clotted heads slept
    in the plastering slime.
And then the rain began, –
    the jolly old rain!

A yawning soldier knelt
    against the bank,

Staring across the morning
   blear with fog;
He wondered when the
   Allemands would get
   busy;
And then, of course, they
   started with five-nines
Traversing, such as fate,
   and never a dud.
Mute in the clamour of
   shells he watched them
   burst

Spouting dark earth and
    wire with gusts from hell,
While posturing giants
    dissolved in drifts of
    smoke.
He crouched and flinched,
    dizzy with galloping fear,
Sick for escape, – loathing
    the strangled horror
And butchered, frantic
    gestures of the dead.

An officer came blundering
    down the trench:
'Stand-to and man the
    fire-step!' On he went . . .
Grasping and bawling,
    'Fire-step . . . counter-
    attack!'
Then the haze lifted.
    Bombing on the right
Down the old sap: machine-
    guns on the left;
And stumbling figures
    looming out in front.

'O Christ, they're coming at
    us!' Bullets spat,
And he remembered his rifle
    ... rapid fire ...
And started blazing wildly ...
    then a bang
Crumpled and spun him
    sideways, knocked him out
To grunt and wriggle: none
    heeded him; he choked

And fought the flapping veils
　　of smothering gloom,
Lost in a blurred confusion
　　of yells and groans . . .
Down, and down, and down,
　　he sank and drowned,
Bleeding to death. The
　　counter-attack had failed.
—1918

Dreamers
Siegfried Sassoon

Soldiers are citizens of
 death's gray land,
Drawing no dividend from
 time's to-morrows.
In the great hour of destiny
 they stand,
Each with his feuds, and
 jealousies, and sorrows.
Soldiers are sworn to
 action; they must win

Some flaming, fatal climax
   with their lives.
Soldiers are dreamers;
   when the guns begin
They think of firelit homes,
   clean beds, and wives.

I see them in foul dug-outs,
   gnawed by rats,
And in the ruined trenches,
   lashed with rain,
Dreaming of things they did
   with balls and bats,

And mocked by hopeless
    longing to regain
Bank-holidays, and picture
    shows, and spats,
And going to the office in
    the train.
—1918

Prelude:
The Troops
Siegfried Sassoon

Dim, gradual thinning of
    the shapeless gloom
Shudders to drizzling
    daybreak that reveals
Disconsolate men who
    stamp their sodden boots
And turn dulled, sunken
    faces to the sky

Haggard and hopeless.
   They, who have beaten
   down
The stale despair of night,
   must now renew
Their desolation in the
   truce of dawn,
Murdering the livid hours
   that grope for peace.

Yet these, who cling to life
   with stubborn hands,

Can grin through storms of
    death and find a gap
In the clawed, cruel tangles
    of his defence.
They march from safety,
    and the bird-sung joy
Of grass-green thickets, to
    the land where all
Is ruin, and nothing
    blossoms but the sky
That hastens over them
    where they endure

Sad, smoking, flat horizons,
    reeking woods,
And foundered trench-lines
    volleying doom for doom.

❖ ❖ ❖

O my brave brown
    companions, when your
    souls
Flock silently away, and the
    eyeless dead
Shame the wild beast of
    battle on the ridge,

Death will stand grieving in
    that field of war
Since your unvanquished
    hardihood is spent.
And through some mooned
    Valhalla there will pass
Battalions and battalions,
    scarred from hell;
The unreturning army that
    was youth;
The legions who have
    suffered and are dust.
—1918

The Rear-Guard
Siegfried Sassoon

Groping along the tunnel,
  step by step,
He winked his prying torch
  with patching glare
From side to side, and sniffed
  the unwholesome air.

❖ ❖ ❖

Tins, boxes, bottles, shapes
  too vague to know,

A mirror smashed, the
　　mattress from a bed;
And he, exploring fifty feet
　　below
The rosy gloom of battle
　　overhead.

Tripping, he grabbed the
　　wall; saw some one lie
Humped at his feet,
　　half-hidden by a rug,
And stooped to give the
　　sleeper's arm a tug,

"I'm looking for
   headquarters," No reply,
"God blast your neck!" (For
   days he'd had no sleep.)

"Get up and guide me
   through this stinking
   place."
Savage, he kicked a soft,
   unanswering heap,
And flashed his beam across
   the livid face

Terribly glaring up, whose
    eyes yet wore
Agony dying hard ten days
    before;
And fists of fingers clutched
    a blackening wound.

❖ ❖ ❖

Alone he staggered on until
    he found
Dawn's ghost that filtered
    down a shafted stair
To the dazed, muttering
    creatures underground

Who hear the boom of
    shells in muffled sound.
At last, with sweat of horror
    in his hair,
He climbed through
    darkness to the twilight
    air,
Unloading hell behind him
    step by step.
—1918

Edgell Rickword
(1898–1982)

Moonrise over Battlefield
Edgell Rickword

After the fallen sun the
  wind was sad
like violins behind immense
  old walls.

Trees were musicians
      swaying round the bed
of a woman in gloomy halls.

❖ ❖ ❖

In privacy of music she
      made ready
with comb and silver dust
      and fard;
under her silken vest her
      little belly
shone like a bladder of
      sweet lard.

She drifted with the grand
   air of a punk
on Heaven's streets
   soliciting white saints;
then lay in bright
   communion on a
   cloud-bank
as one who near extreme of
   pleasure faints.

Then I thought, standing in
   the ruined trench,

(all around, dead Boche
   white-shirted lay like
   sheep),
'Why does this damned
   entrancing bitch
seek lovers only among
   them that sleep?'
—1921

The Soldier Addresses His Body

Edgell Rickword

I shall be mad if you get
   smashed about,
We've had good times
   together, you and I;
Although you groused a bit
   when luck was out,
And women passionless,
   and we went dry.

Yet there are many things
  we have not done;
Countries not seen, where
  people do strange things;
Eat fish alive, and mimic in
  the sun
The solemn gestures of
  their stone-grey kings.

I've heard of forests that are
  dim at noon
Where snakes and creepers
  wrestle all day long;

Where vivid beasts grow
    pale with the full moon,
Gibber and cry, and wail a
    mad old song;

❖ ❖ ❖

Because at the full moon
    the Hippogriff,
With crinkled ivory snout
    and agate feet,
With his green eyes will
    glare them cold and stiff
For the coward Wyvern to
    come down and eat.

❖ ❖ ❖

Vodka and kvass, and bitter
   mountain wines
We have not drunk, nor
   snatched at bursting
   grapes
To pelt slim girls along
   Sicilian vines
Who'd flicker through the
   leaves, faint frolic shapes.

Yes, there are many things
  we have not done,
But it's a sweat to knock
  them into rhyme,
Let's have a drink, and give
  the cards a run
And leave dull verse to the
  dull peaceful time.
—1921

War and Peace
Edgell Rickword

In sodden trenches I have
   heard men speak,
Though numb and
   wretched, wise and witty
   things;
And loved them for the
   stubbornness that clings
Longest to laughter when
   Death's pulleys creak;

And seeing cool nurses
    move on tireless feet
To do abominable things
    with grace,
Deemed them sweet sisters
    in that haunted place
Where, with child's voices,
    strong men howl or bleat.

❖ ❖ ❖

Yet now those men lay
    stubborn courage by,
Riding dull-eyed and silent
    in the train

To old men's stools; or sell
    gay-coloured socks
And listen fearfully for
    Death; so I
Love the low-laughing girls,
    who now again
Go daintily, in thin and
    flowery frocks.
—1921

Herbert Read
(1893–1968)

The Retreat
Herbert Read

When in some sudden hush
   of earth
The pulsing rhythm is lost,
   and I am alone

With all those melancholy
    forces of the mind
That wait for empty
    moments, with no sound
Of living wings, or vocal
    throats, or any of the
    subtle
Crepitations that betray
The sense in things—when
    in some sudden hush
I fall victim to the ghouls
I buried years ago in
    sepulcher

Of calm amnesia then once
     more
I see the screen the years
     have built
Between this day and the
     patterns wrought
In love and battle by the
     ecstatic heart.
And again I strive
To hold the real design of
     life
Within the intenser

Light of the mind in these
    moments. I cannot tell
If this calm be illusion; or if
The fiendish days were real.
I know that then I lived
Like the clean movement of
    a wheel
Flying on so fair an axle that
    the eye
Can hardly make its
    motion. The mind was
    absent then

Or but a mirror, passively
   receiving
The body's ritual –a body
   that would glide
On quivering wings, against
   the sun,
And never note
The world that lay beneath,
   pensive with agony.

But now, the world is real
   and calm:
The body lives, a limp
   container
Of this bounding mind;
And the mind notes the
   visible world—
How it moves with
   mechanic evenness,
Dismissing hope and hasty
   exaltations.
The mind is melancholy,
   and frets

On all the futile longingness
   of men,
Their fantasies and
   thought-selected dreams.

❖ ❖ ❖

I hold a little to the living
   earth,
Now so quiescent;
I hold no less to that mental
   life
I would at least in fancy
Mingle with the base of
   things—

Not mind and matter,
 co-distinct
In man alone, or alone in
 living things
But a tympanum for the
 rhythms of ether,
An element
Incarnate in everything.
 Life is but a lesser lesion
Of this extensive energy,
 and so life is less
A thing to wonder at and
 worship—

Is but one mechanism more
    to manifest the force
Active even in the gulfs of
    uncreated space.

So let these agonies, wrung
    from the utterly fragile
Frame of human life, be at
    rest,
Perspectively doomed and
    wrought
To the little loudness of an
    insect's cry.

What matter now
The mind's phantom
  inquisitors?
What if they unleash the
  blood-loving hounds
And all the unlimited woes
  of hate?
These echo faintly in the
  corridors
Carved cavernously
  wherever the mind
Looks down into the waste
  of stars.

Liberty and power, and that
    light-winged joy
That is the folly of
    forgetfulness,
These do not come in the
    unguarded
Moods of quiet. At that time
The unhealing features of
    the brain
Revive their dim wounds, to
    burn, to bleed,
To flow with the lava of
    thought's lucid pain.

Oh, turn your milk dim eyes
To outer things! See where
  a haze
Trembles against the hard
  horizon,
Quivering in a rhythm that
  calls to mind
The ultimate harmony of
  the world!
The same rhythm
Governs the structure of all
  that's seen

And felt and heard—of all
    that's known
In the deep percipient heart
    of man.
This mind alone, like a rock
Rebounding
    disharmoniously down
    some precipice
Is carried by unconscious
    force
Till death give it inertia.

But the same mind has seen
Beauties beyond its reach,
   perfections
Never to be attained. Some
   state of high serenity
Exists beyond the range.
Of febrile senses.
The starved heart sickens
In longingness, and from
   the sickness
Emerges the troubled drift
   of men. The past,

Now like a riot of dreamy
    horror,
Is this heart's sickness, and
    its diurnal function.

The still day; a river at my
    feet;
And the yellow leaf that
    flags
In the calm cincture of the
    hollowed bank—
These and all percipient
    joys,

These are the dreamland
   state.
We wake to conflict: the
   mind is in a prison
With a high small window,
   barred against escape.
A decoy of light enters
   there,
Reminding the tortured
   brain that somewhere
   unseen
The wide perfection of the
   sun's way exists.

Beyond time and space
    there is a beauty
Not to be seized by men in
    prison, who but languish
In shackles carried from the
    womb, and worn
Unto the release of death:
    unto the dark return
Of world's harmony.
—1919

Thomas Hardy
(1840-1928)

Men Who March Away
(Song of the Soldiers)
Thomas Hardy

What of the faith and
   fire within us
Men who march away

Ere the barn-cocks say
Night is growing gray,
To hazards whence no tears
   can win us;
What of the faith and fire
   within us
Men who march away!

❖ ❖ ❖

Is it a purblind prank,
   O think you,
Friend with the musing eye
Who watch us stepping by
With doubt and dolorous
   sigh?

Can much pondering so
   hoodwink you?
Is it a purblind prank,
   O think you,
Friend with the musing
   eye?

❖❖❖

Nay. We see well what we
   are doing,
Though some may not see –
Dalliers as they be –
England's need are we;
Her distress would leave
   us rueing:

Thomas Hardy

Nay. We will see what we
    are doing,
Though some may not see!

❖ ❖ ❖

In our heart of hearts
    believing
Victory crowns the just,
And that braggarts must
Surely bite the dust,
Press we to the field
    ungrieving,
In our heart of hearts
    believing

Victory crowns the just.

❖ ❖ ❖

Hence the faith and fire
    within us
Men who march away
Ere the barn-cocks say
Night is growing gray,
To hazards whence no tears
    can win us;
Hence the faith and fire
    within us
Men who march away.
—1914

And There Was a Great Calm

(On The Signing of the Armistice November 11, 1918)

Thomas Hardy

There had been years of
 Passion—scorching, cold,
And much Despair, and
 Anger heaving high,
Care whitely watching;
 Sorrows manifold,

Among the young, among
   the weak and old,
And the pensive Spirit of
   Pity whispered, 'Why?'

❖ ❖ ❖

Men had not paused to
   answer. Foes distraught
Pierced the thinned peoples
   in a brute-like blindness,
Philosophies that sages
   long had taught,

And Selflessness, were as an
    unknown thought,
And 'Hell!' and 'Shell!' were
    yapped at Lovingkindness.

❖ ❖ ❖

The feeble folk at home had
    grown full-used
To 'dug-outs,' 'snipers,'
    'Huns,' from the war-adept
In the morning heard, and at
    evetides perused;

To day-dreamt men in
   millions when they
   mused—
To nightmare-men in
   millions when they slept.

❖ ❖ ❖

Waking to wish existence
   timeless, null,
Sirius they watched above
   where armies fell;
He seemed to check his
   flapping when, in the lull

Of night a boom came
    thencewise, like the dull
Plunge of a stone dropped
    into some deep well.

❖ ❖ ❖

So, when old hopes that earth
    was bettering slowly
Were dead and dammed,
    there sounded 'War is
    done!'
One morrow. Said the bereft,
    and meek, and lowly,

'Will men some day be given
    to grace? Yea, wholly,
And in good sooth, as our
    dreams used to run?'

Breathless they paused.
    Out there men raised
    their glance
To where had stood those
    poplars lank and lopped,
As they had raised it through
    the four years' dance

Of Death in the now
　　familiar flats of France;
And murmured, 'Strange,
　　this! How? All firing
　　stopped?'

❖ ❖ ❖

Aye; all was hushed. The
　　about-to-fire fired not,
The aimed-at moved away
　　in trance-lipped song.
One checkless regiment
　　slung a clinching shot

And turned. The Spirit of
   Irony smirked out,
      'What?
Spoil peradventures woven
   of Rage and Wrong?'

❖ ❖ ❖

Thenceforth no flying fires
   inflamed the gray,
No hurtlings shook the
   dewdrop from the thorn,
No moan perplexed the
   mute bird on the spray;

Worn horses mused: 'We
    are not whipped to-day';
No weft-winged engines
    blurred the moon's
    thin horn.

Calm fell. From Heaven
    distilled a clemency;
There was peace on earth,
    and silence in the sky;
Some could, some could
    not, shake off misery:

The Sinister Spirit sneered:
    'It had to be!'
And again the Spirit of Pity
    whispered, 'Why?'
—1920

Credits

Photos:

58–59, 218: Courtesy of
Everett Collection

Poems:

We would like to acknowledge the
following publishers and individ-
uals for permission to reprint the
following material. Every effort has
been made to obtain permission
from the appropriate parties to
include these works, but if any
errors have been made we will be
happy to correct them.

"August, 1914" reprinted by permission of the Society of Authors as the Literary Representative of the Estate of John Masefield.

"The Retreat" from *Collected Poems* (1966), published by Faber & Faber. Reprinted by permission of David Hingham Associates.

"Moonrise over Battlefield", "The Soldier Addresses His Body", and "War and Peace" from *Collected Poems* (1991). Reprinted by permission of Carcanet Press Limited.

This book has been bound using
handcraft methods and Smyth-
sewn to ensure durability.

The dust jacket was designed by
Amanda Richmond.

The interior was designed by
Matthew Goodman.

The text was edited by
Geoffrey Stone.

The text was set in
Chronicle and Whitney.